Breaking the Chains

Living Beyond Defeat

_____

Bonnie Wagner

Breaking the Chains
Published by Total Fusion Press
6475 Cherry Run Rd. Strasburg, OH 44680
www.totalfusionpress.com

ISBN-10: 0988370093
ISBN-13: 978-0-9883700-9-8

Library of Congress Control Number: 2014937714

Cover Design by Abby Smith
Edited by Andrea Long
Interior Design by Linnette Hayden

Scriptures are taken from the KING JAMES VERSION (KJV): KING JAMES VERSION, public domain.

Published in Association with Total Fusion Ministries, Strasburg, OH.
www.totalfusionministries.org

Dedication

I would like to dedicate this book first and for most to Jesus Christ who is the author and finisher of my life. He has restored, renewed and given me a purpose for everything in my life. In the good times and the bad it is well with my soul, for He has led me to my Father and given me an eternal home.

To my earthly father Dominick Blanda who has gone to his eternal home. You were my rock and taught me to love, care and encourage me to believe in myself. He gave me a glimpse of my father in heaven and his unconditional love.

Table of Contents

Introduction

Have you ever looked at the faces of people in society today? Have you noticed all the headlines in the paper and on the evening news? The people of today are lost in a world of lies and deception. People are searching for an antidote to the hopelessness that lurks in every corner of the world.

So many people live in their own worlds of defeat, feeling lost, and lacking hope of ever rising above it. Defeat allows one to fall into the snare of false remedies and quick fixes. There are so many people who walk around with addictions, pain, suffering, anger, bitterness, low self-esteem, depression—and if you take a minute, I would guess you could name about a million more struggles to add to this list.

You can go to any bookstore and find books that will teach you how to become rich, how to manage your money, how to find happiness. This is not one of those books. This is a book of *movement*: a movement to bring hope, encouragement, strength, and truth. This movement will move you out of the agony of defeat and into victory by growing you in a relationship with Jesus Christ—a relationship that consists of depending upon the Holy Spirit and living in the truth of God. This will bring life change and transformation to your world. The movement will become a part of who you are, rather than just changing what you do. This movement will take time. You cannot rush through the process, and you cannot fake it—you must fall in love with the person of Jesus as you journey into a lifestyle of victory.

Today you are embarking on a journey that will change your life forever. This day you will begin to transform defeat and begin to move into victory. You will begin to experience the power of living a life that is not lived in defeat, but rather in victory and power! Are you ready to break the chains that hold you captive in the darkness of defeat? It is time to experience a movement that will carry you into a relationship with the Almighty God that empowers you toward a lifestyle of victorious living!

To experience this movement, you must be willing to discipline yourself to do whatever it takes to live beyond the foothold of defeat. Will you push yourself and move closer to God, expecting a life-changing breakthrough? There can be no excuses. This is not a religion, a program, or a self-help book; but a powerful, supernatural encounter with the Holy Spirit and His transforming power! This is not a book to help you accumulate knowledge. This is a journey to receive power to pull down strongholds and overcome the spirit of defeat. This journey will begin to move you into a relationship with a living, supernatural God. This relationship will transform hopelessness into hope, fear into courage, and defeat into victory. Victory is only obtained by the presence and power of the Holy Spirit.

Before you begin, please understand that your circumstances may not change. This is not a fix-the-negative-situation book. This is a book that leads you into a *heart* change even when the circumstance is not changing or going to change. The change begins by having a heart connection with the power of God, surrendering to the cross of Jesus Christ, and allowing the Spirit of God to transform your heart attitude. If you surrender your heart, you will enter into a heart of joy no matter what your circumstance may be.

This book will coach you through the life changes. It will provide scripture, disciplines, exercises called Life Changers, and encouragement for the soul. Most of all, it will provide you with strategies to connect deeper with the Almighty God, breaking your chains of sin and trouble, and living beyond the world's defeat.

ARE YOU READY?
LET'S BEGIN!

Autobiography

My name is Bonnie Wagner. I am delighted that you are ready to break the chains and live beyond defeat. God has amazing doors and mysteries He wants to unlock and reveal to you. He wants to set the captives free. He wants you to live in the power of His victory.

In my life I have raised four daughters, and now enjoy my grandchildren. I served on staff at a church for seventeen years as the Director of Ministries until God called me into the next season of my life. I have been married to my best friend, Dan, for over thirty years. Together we have traveled a road of adversity. With this adversity, we have shared joys, sorrows, tears, and triumphs. Along the road of difficulties, God continually showed His mercy and grace. He revealed His hand was upon us with each curve in the road. While raising our children, we encountered a war zone. The battles we had fought were as follows:

- A child with bulimia
- A child with epilepsy
- A child engaged in witchcraft
- A child with alcohol and drug addiction
- A child convicted of a felony
- Two teen pregnancies
- Two divorced children
- A child's sexual promiscuity (due to low self-esteem)
- A marriage divided (Dan and I live two different lifestyles, each with our own belief systems)

- The death of a father
- Two bankruptcies
- A severe blood disorder

This is just the short version. For more information on this list, I recommend reading *Conquer and Conquest*, my written testimony of the adversities, joys, tears and struggles of my life. If you struggle with a divided marriage, please read more about mine in *Divided We Stand*, my second book.

The journey through those years was difficult and often painful. Through the storm, God held tightly to our hands. He never left or abandoned us. Together God and my family met and rose above every storm. He walked with us through each adversity and led us on to victory. Satan strategized hard to keep us in a heart of defeat, but God wanted victory! What Satan tried to bring upon us, God reversed to bring hope, restoration, and growth. I would have never made it through the attacks on our lives without the power and relationship of the one true God. God is with you through the storm. He longs to show you that He is in control, and to reveal His presence.

The Word

"For I know the thoughts that I think toward you, saith the Lord, thoughts of peace, and not of evil, to give you an expected end." - Jeremiah 29:11

How to Use this Guide

- This book is organized into sections, not chapters, that each lead to a transformational assignment called a Life Changer.
- Move slowly at your own pace. Do not hurry. Pray and meditate on each Life Changer.
- Prayerfully consider each question in your heart. Some blank pages are provided for your journaling after each Life Changer. Please utilize this space to answer questions, record your thoughts, or write out prayers.
- Complete each Life Changer exercise, keeping in mind that you are not striving to fill in the blanks. You are entering into a deeper relationship with Jesus Christ.

Remember, this is NOT a curriculum or a program. This is a movement that will take you into a heart relationship with God. Just going through the motions will not bring the power of God. *Life change* means exactly what it says: changing the way you live your life. Seeking God and surrendering your heart is the key to each of the life changes that you will be asked to complete.

As a personal life coach, I can walk with you through these life-changing steps. For more information or to connect with me to become your life coach, contact me at my personal email address: bswags44@sssnet.com

Before you begin this life-changing experience, understand this may only assist in some more difficult issues. In some cases you may need to seek professional help or other useful programs to help overcome your defeat. This is not by any means a medical or counseling book. This is a book that moves you into a dynamic relationship with God. If any of the following issues are what you are experiencing, please seek additional help:

- Severe depression
- Anxiety
- Addictions
- Suicidal tendencies
- Eating disorders
- Self-harm, or self-destructive behaviors
- Uncontrollable anger
- Marital issues

If you have these or any other severe issues or disorders, please seek out help. Have a professional assess the problem, and then move on with this journey.

Prayer

Lord, today I begin my journey with You. Please open my eyes that I may see. Please open my heart that it may be molded by Your hand. This will be a difficult journey. God, help me to depend on You and not my own will. Lord, when things begin to get tough, help me to be strong. I no longer want to live in the world of defeat. I want to live in the joy of victory. Help me to trust you, Lord. Break my will and mold it to Yours.

In Jesus' Name, _____

Amen

The Fall of Man into Sin

God had created man with the intent that he would live in a perfect world. Man was supposed to live in a world where God himself provided for our needs and walked in a relationship with us. God created man and placed him in a garden. This garden was beautiful. The garden had every kind of tree that was not only pleasing to the eye, but also good for food. God loved man—and man and God were not separated.

Read Genesis Chapters 1-2, and then consider the following questions (remember to utilize the blank pages, if you desire):

1) How did God create man?

2) Why did God create woman?

3) Where did God place man?

4) What did God instruct man to *not* do?

5) What did God say would happen if man disobeyed?

God placed Adam and Eve in the garden free of pain, and free of turmoil. The garden was a place of perfect peace and provision. God provided all they would ever need and He gave them a command: *Do not touch or eat of the tree of wisdom or you will surely die.*

Read Genesis Chapter 3 and then consider the following questions:

6) Who spoke to the woman?

7) What was said to the woman?

8) What did the woman choose to do?

9) What happened after they ate from the forbidden tree?

10) When they heard the Lord walking in the garden, what did they do?

11) What happened to the perfect world after man and woman disobeyed God?

Man was created in a sinless, perfect world; but free will of choice moved him from a perfect world of peace and provision into a tarnished world of sin and strife. Disobedience turned the wheel of sin, and death into motion:

- Adam and Eve were told not to eat of a certain tree. In their disobedience, they ate from it anyway.
- God asked them why they ate of the fruit, but they lied and blamed it on others.

- Adam and Eve had a choice of right and wrong—they chose wrong, which led to sin and death.
- Because of this sin, they hid from God—separating them from His presence.

Because of Adam and Eve's choice to disobey God, sin entered into the human race for every man, woman, and child that would follow after them. Man is born into sin, and must now choose between right and wrong. Too often, man now chooses lies from the serpent as Eve did, instead of the truth God continues to provide. Man hides from the Lord and separates himself from truth. Death and sin are now the productivity which man has chosen.

You live in a fallen world, a world of decay and corruption due to sin. This is the consequence that man must endure because of his decisions.

Romans 6:23a "For the wages of sin is death..."

Man is spiritually dead due to the sin in his life. God did not create man to be separated from Him, but to have fellowship and unity with Him. God is a holy God—pure and perfect, without blemish. He cannot look upon man with sin hovering over him. God had to make a way for man to be reconciled to Him. God needed a perfect, unblemished sacrifice to pay for the wages of sin. God gave man the perfect sacrifice in Jesus Christ.

2 Timothy 3:16 "**All scripture is given by inspiration of God, and is profitable for doctrine, for reproof, for correction, for instruction in righteousness.**"

2 Peter 1:21 "**For the prophecy came not in old time by the will of man: but holy men of God spake as they were moved by the Holy Ghost.**"

12) According to 2 Timothy, who inspired the Word of God?

13) For what is scripture profitable?

14) Define the following words:
Doctrine
Reproof
Correction
Instruction
Righteousness

15) 2 Peter says men of God were moved by whom?

The Bible is inspired by God and written by God. The Bible is the ultimate authority. The Word is truth. This truth leads, instructs, corrects, and teaches us how to overcome and live a victorious lifestyle through the power of the living God. The Word of God gives hope, strength, redemption, and will teach you how to live a godly lifestyle. This Word was not written by the world's standards or views.

The world lives by standards of right and wrong, which are not necessarily God's standards.

Hebrews 4:12 "For the word of God is quick, and powerful, and sharper than any two-edged sword, piercing even to the dividing asunder of soul and spirit, and of the joints and marrow, and is a discerner of the thoughts and intents of the heart."

16) What is the Word of God?

17) What does the Word of God pierce?

18) What does the Word of God discern?

For many years you may have formed your behavior and thoughts according to the world's point of view. Many of those thoughts and actions are not in line with the truth of the Word of God. Habits have been formed. Thoughts have been burned into your heart and mind. The Word of God will pierce into your very lifestyle and do what 2 Timothy promises. This process is called *transformation*. The Word of God is what transforms or affirms your thoughts, actions, and purpose. The Word of God pierces your very soul. Without the Word of God you have no means to compare your thoughts and actions. You are unable to know truth, real love, or the difference between right and wrong.
Read John Chapter 8.

Satan wants you to live out the lies with which he entices you. Satan is the father of lies, and he exchanges God's truth for his deception. When you allow Satan to fill your heart with lies, Satan then feeds off of those lies to spiral you down into a deeper chasm of defeat.

God wants you to have the complete opposite experience. God wants you to live in victory and freedom. He wants truth to be lived and believed in all people. The Word exposes all of Satan's lies that bring destruction. The truth is revealed so that you may choose to exchange the devil's lies for God's ultimate truth. The world does not have God's truth, nor does the world live by it. Because the world does not live by truth, it plays directly into the destructive hands of Satan. Satan then is able to keep shackling men into his bondage of chains.

Society cries out through magazines and commercials: *spend, use credit cards, buy, buy, and continue buying! The one with the most toys wins!* This mindset creates bondage to debt. This bondage causes many good people financial ruin because of overspending. But God's truth, His written Word, speaks a different message.

Proverbs 22:7 "The rich ruleth over the poor, and the borrower is servant to the lender."

Proverbs 22:26 "Be not thou one of them that strike hands, or of them that are sureties for debts."

The translation of this scripture is basically that if you owe money, you are slave to the one you owe.

Spending money frivolously and with credit will only bring calamity. If the world lived according to the truth, no one would be in bankruptcy court or stressing about credit card bills. The world would have a peaceful handle on their finances.

The written Word reveals truth in all situations. With the truth comes correction, knowledge, conviction, and if you choose to embrace the truth—transformation. If you embrace truth, with it comes victory and freedom.

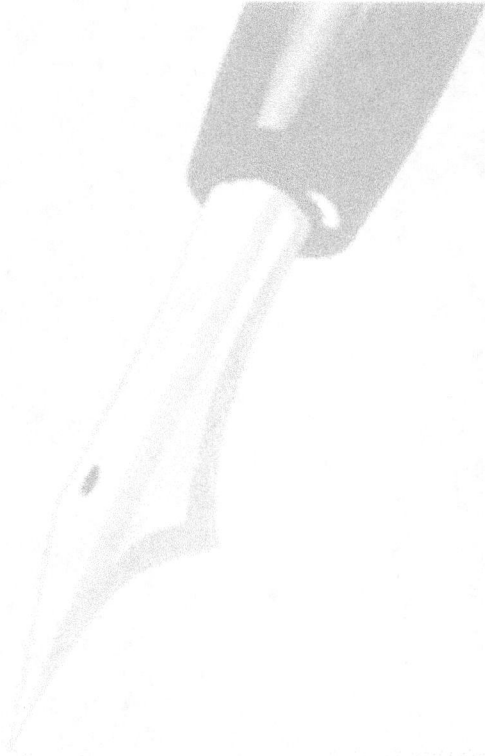

Our Need, Our Savior

Since sin crept into our world, all of mankind has had a need for a Savior. Man must be saved from a spiritual death that will keep him separated from God for eternity. God has met our need by giving us a Savior in Jesus Christ. Without Jesus, man would be separated from God forever. Without Jesus, when man passes from this life to the next—and there *is* a next life—he will pass into an eternity of hell. Man has a decision: to accept Jesus as his Savior, or accept sin, thereby rejecting Jesus. This decision ultimately determines man's final destination. There is not *one* human being who is righteous on his own. All men experience sin, and therefore need a Savior.

Romans 3:10 "As it is written, There is none righteous, no, not one"

Romans 3:23 "For all have sinned, and come short of the glory of God"

Read Chapters 1-4 in the book of Romans, then consider the following questions:

1) The wrath of God applies to whom?

2) Why did God give man up to his own desires?

3) What does it mean to give up?

25

4) For what does man exchange the truth of God?

5) How many humans have sinned?

Man chooses to follow after his own desires. God allows man to follow those desires, for He has given us free will. If you have only sinned one time in your life, that is enough to keep you separated from God for all of eternity.

Romans 6:23 "For the wages of sin is death; but the gift of God is eternal life through Jesus Christ our Lord."

Use Romans 6:23 to respond to the following questions:

6) What are the wages of sin?

7) What is God's gift?

8) Through whom do you receive this gift?

At this point you may be asking, *"What does all this have to do with what I am battling?"* In response, I tell you this: Jesus and the power of His Spirit is the only key to unlock your circumstance and open the gateway to freedom and victory. If Jesus is not the center of your life—if He is not Lord of your life—you cannot have truth, nor will you understand truth. Defeat is a lie in your life provided by the devil, who is a great liar. Truth is the *only* weapon to combat defeat. Truth can only be found in *Jesus Christ*, who gave His life to come and set the captives free.

Luke 4:18 "The Spirit of the Lord is upon me, because he hath anointed me to preach the gospel to the poor; he hath sent me to heal the brokenhearted, to preach deliverance to the captives, and recovering of sight to the blind, to set at liberty them that are bruised"

You are held captive by sin, and the power of Jesus is the only hope of freedom from this captivity. Society's morals and conduct are not abiding in God's truth. Man perceives what he has seen, been taught, and experiences as truth; but the truth of the world does not line up with the truth of God's written Word.

Here is an example: *People believe that vengeance is their right. If someone wrongs another, we think it is alright to retaliate. Retaliation is justified: after all, that person harmed you, so they deserve payback for that harm.* This way of thinking breeds so many horrible crimes that people commit against each other.

God's truth is a little different than our own worldly thinking:

Matthew 18:21-22 "(21) Then came Peter to him, and said, Lord, how oft shall my brother sin against me, and I forgive him? Till seven

times? (22) Jesus saith unto him, I say not unto thee, until seven times: but, until seventy times seven."

Truth in God can only be found when one surrenders to Jesus.

John 14:16 "Jesus saith unto him, I am the way, the truth, and the life: no man cometh unto the Father, but by me."

John 1:1 "In the beginning was the Word, and the Word was with God, and the Word was God."

John 14:6 explains very clearly the way to the Father, through Jesus, the truth and the life. There is no other access or gateway found to enter into these gates. You must enter in by the blood of the Lamb and the name of Jesus.

Look at John 1:1. Why is *the Word* capitalized each time? Capitalization, unless you are beginning a new sentence—which is clearly not the case here—signifies a proper name. The proper name for the Word here can be substituted with the name of Jesus. The Word and Jesus are two names referring to the same person. Jesus is God, living out the Word of God and the Word is truth.

God orchestrated a perfect plan to reunite man with Him. God wanted to bring man to the original place for which He created him. Jesus—God Himself, the

Word, the Truth, the Way—became the perfect sacrifice needed to cover man's sin.

Please read the following scripture passages, and then answer the questions below:

John 3:16 "For God so loved the world, that he gave his only begotten Son, that whosoever believeth in him should not perish, but have everlasting life."

Acts 4:12 "Neither is there salvation in any other: for there is none other name under heaven given among men, whereby we must be saved."

Romans 5:8 "But God commendeth his love toward us, in that, while we were yet sinners, Christ died for us."

Romans 10:9 "That if thou shalt confess with thy mouth the Lord Jesus, and shalt believe in thine heart that God hath raised him from the dead, thou shalt be saved."

9) In John 3:16, who loved the world?

10) What did God give to the world?

11) What must one do to not perish?

12) What does it mean to believe with your heart?

13) If one believes, what does one receive?

14) John 14:6 names three doorways that Jesus claims to be. What are they?

15) In Romans 5:8, who died for you and what were you doing while he died?

16) In your own words, what does it mean to *confess*?

17) What must one confess, according to Romans 10:9?

➤ LIFE CHANGER #1

Remember this is not a program or a to-do book. Throughout this text, we will pause for a LIFE CHANGER exercise, as our goal is to experience a life change that moves you from religion to relationship with a powerful and living God. Are you ready for the transformation? Ask yourself these personal questions: *"Have I surrendered my life to Jesus, and what does surrender mean? Have I surrendered with just words, or also with my heart? Do I follow a religion, or truly have a relationship with Jesus Christ? Is my relationship with Christ built on His truth—that He is the Way, the Truth, and the Life?"*

To find the truth, life, and way, you must surrender all to Christ. If your attitude of defeat is going to transform, your heart must be surrendered to the work of Jesus and His truth. That will start the process of setting you free from the chains. Truth is the only power to break the cycle of bondage.

1) On a journal page, make a list of all your sins, past and present. Take some time to really think about this.

2) Along with the list of sins, jot down any negative emotions or thoughts you have had in your heart.

Reading what you have written, do you believe these are truly sins, and that you are in need of a Savior? Those sins have separated you from God. Those sins, if not forgiven, have determined your

31

eternal destination—separation from God forever in hell. Jesus walked to Calvary to nail your sin—that list—to the cross once and for all, reuniting you back with God. Do you believe in the work of the cross? Have you totally surrendered your life to His truth and His way? Have you ever called upon the name of Jesus to forgive you and to take Lordship of your life? Read Romans 10:9 once again, and then consider the following:

1) What must one confess with?

Using one's mouth means *to speak it into existence.*

Surrender means *to declare yourself defeated, or to give up possession.*

Now put these two actions together: *speak in your own words that you surrender your life to Jesus Christ. Declare you are defeated and have lived life on your own terms. Give your life to Jesus. Admit that your sins need to be forgiven, and invite Jesus to become the Truth in your life. Surrender and confess that Jesus Christ is Lord!*

If you cannot surrender with a heart-felt conviction and confess the need for Jesus to be Lord of your life, then do not proceed. Seek after the meaning of what you have read thus far. Ask God to open your eyes to see Jesus, and give you clarity before you continue on this journey.

Without Jesus, you cannot have a life-changing relationship.

Prayer

Lord, I thank You for Your Son. I praise You for making a way for me to be reunited with You. I am a child of the King and for that I thank You. As You gave Your very best for me, I would now like to give my best to You. Teach me Your ways. Guide me in the path of righteousness. Guide my path to where You would have me walk and grow in the knowledge of who You are and what my purpose is for the Kingdom.

In Jesus' Name,

Amen

Journal Page ─────────────────────────

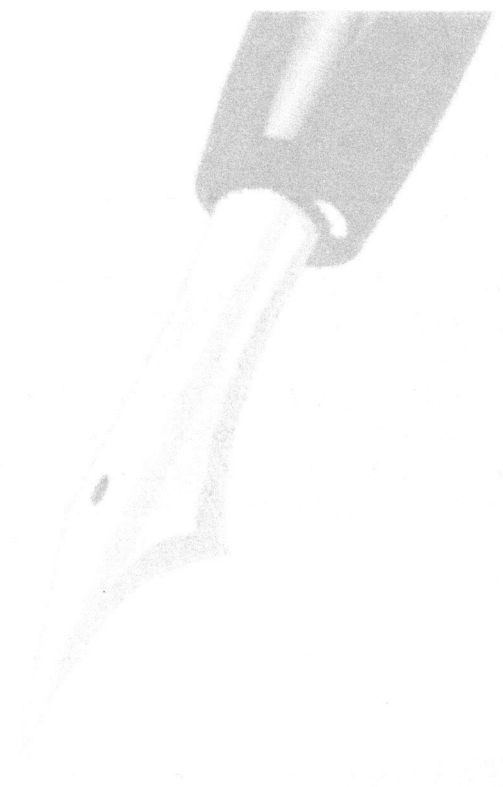

A Tie that Binds

If you have proceeded on this journey, I will assume you have fully surrendered to Jesus. You are now a child of the King! With this life change, you have now entered into a realm where all things will become new. You are a changed person. You may not feel different or look different, but you are a new creation!

2 Corinthians 5:17 "Therefore if any man be in Christ, he is a new creature: old things are passed away; behold all things are become new."

As you begin your journey into truth, revelations will start to pierce your soul. You will begin to have a heart change in the way you have perceived your worldview. The lies the enemy has told you will start to be exchanged for the truth of God's Word. God is always with you. You are never alone.

Hebrews 13:5b "...I will never leave thee, nor forsake thee."

You will need flesh and blood to uplift and encourage you to continue with your new walk and relationship with Jesus. As I said, this earth does not live by God's truth—you simply will not find it anywhere in the world. You must go where truth can be found, and is lived and taught. You must live among other believers who stand on the same truth. And where do believers gather? You will find them in your local church!

If you are not already connected with a body of believers, it is vital that you do so. Every child of God needs to gather with other children. These believers in the local church will become your spiritual family. Many say, *"I don't need to go to church to believe in God."* While that may be partially true, you certainly *do* need to attend church with other believers. There is much more value in a life lived in connection with other believers than there is in just believing in Jesus independently. You need to be deeply rooted in a body of believers who will gather around to cheer you on into living beyond defeat.

Ecclesiastes 4:12 "And if one prevail against him, two shall withstand him; and a threefold cord is not quickly broken."

Hebrews 10:25 "Not forsaking the assembling of ourselves together, as the manner of some is; but exhorting one another: and so much the more, as ye see the day approaching."

The church family provides strength when one is weak. Read the passage from Ecclesiastes again, then I want you to do an object lesson:

- You will need yarn and scissors.
- Cut four pieces of yarn.
- Take three of the pieces and weave or braid them together.
- Take the single remaining yarn and try to break it.
- Now take the braided yarn and try to break it.
- Which was more difficult to break?

The braided cord was stronger when woven together than the one that stood alone. The cord with three strands had two more pieces for reinforcement. It is the same with other believers when they gather together. If one person is left on his own while weak, he may break because there is no one to help, no one to be the strength in the time of weakness, no one to hold him together. If there are two or more people gathering with the weaker strand to provide encouragement and prayer, the weaker strand is able to stand when the difficult tension starts to try and break him. The other two strands are the reinforcement that keeps the weaker strand strong. The body of believers provides strength, support, and encouragement through prayer and friendship.

As you battle the hardships of life, at some point you will become exhausted, discouraged, and weak. Connecting with believers will give you the strength for another day, the courage and support to press forward. Without other believers you become isolated to fight the battle all alone. The enemy wants to isolate you. You have heard that there is strength in numbers. Connecting with a body of believers definitely is your strength in numbers.

The Need to Hear ────────────────

You need to hear God's Word to understand God's divine wisdom on life issues. Frequently hearing from an educated, spirit-filled, Bible-based leader, who is anointed to preach the Word of God, is crucial to your growth. Hearing the Word of God fills one's heart with the light of promise, hope, and redirection for living. Hearing God's Word gives encouragement to keep reaching for the prize of victory.

Romans 10:17 "So then faith cometh by hearing, and hearing by the word of God."

Hebrews 11:1 "Now faith is the substance of things hoped for, the evidence of things not seen."

1) How does faith come?

2) What is faith?

Hearing—absorbing the Word of God—grows your faith to believe and to place hope in the Jesus you are trusting. Hearing God's Word brings hope, power, and energy to continue to believe and live by the written Word. Listening to the Word of God and the testimony which the Word delivers reinforces that God is with you and that He is alive and active and interceding on your behalf. When you start hearing and believing in the power of God, this empowers you to move into His supernatural realm of the Kingdom, and to press on into storming the gates of hell that keep you prisoner. God's Word is food for the soul.

Faith, strength, and hope cannot grow without hearing the message of God.

Meeting Your Needs

I have been connected with my church family since 1991. If I could sum up their strength as a body of believers it would be this: They rise to the occasion to meet the needs of the people.

Right after her high school graduation, my daughter, Nikki, shared that she was pregnant. We had nothing to prepare us for a little baby. I went to church the following Sunday and shared with some of the people of the congregation the news of the new arrival soon to come. Within three weeks, the church gathered a crib, bassinet, swing, car seat, baby sleepers, crib sheets, and blankets. What a blessing!

Acts 2:44-45 "(44) And all that believed were together, and had all things common; (45) And sold their possessions and goods, and parted them to all men, as every man had need."

God may or may not ask believers to sell their possessions, but He definitely calls His people to meet the needs of others. Connecting with a body of believers helps to provide for needs that may occur through a difficult time. The church works together in providing for those needs.

Serving Together —————————————————

Read 1 Corinthians Chapter 12

> 3) In your own words, what is this chapter revealing about the church?

You have a divine purpose. God has given you a supernatural, extraordinary gift to help build His Kingdom. (More will be discussed on this topic later in the book.) Believers gather together to serve people, and to change lives for the Kingdom. Each person, along with the gifts God has given them, provides a place for growing together in power and spirit to bring others into the Kingdom.

Connecting and becoming a part of the church family is not optional. It is a command from God. This is a mandatory discipline given to enhance your relationship with God and with other believers.

Matthew 6:33 "But seek ye first the kingdom of God, and his righteousness; and all these things shall be added unto you."

➢ **LIFE CHANGER #2**

If you are not connected to a local church, research one in your area that teaches Biblical truths (as noted below) and begin attending at least once a week.

Biblical Truths:
- Jesus Christ was God and died on the cross for your sin.
- Jesus Christ arose from the grave on the third day.
- God the Father, God the Son, and God the Spirit are one.
- There is an eternal heaven and hell.
- The Holy Spirit dwells in every believer.

Attend weekly and participate in worship, hear the Word, love the people, and connect to the community of faith.

Prayer

Lord, I thank You for other believers and for allowing me to live in a country that has the freedom to gather for worship. Help me to gather with my spiritual family. Help me to hear Your Word and allow that Word to pierce my heart. As I continue to gather in the body of believers, help me to fall in love with them and begin to understand how You move among them. Never allow me to take what You have given me for granted.

In Jesus' Name,

Amen

Journal Page —————————————————

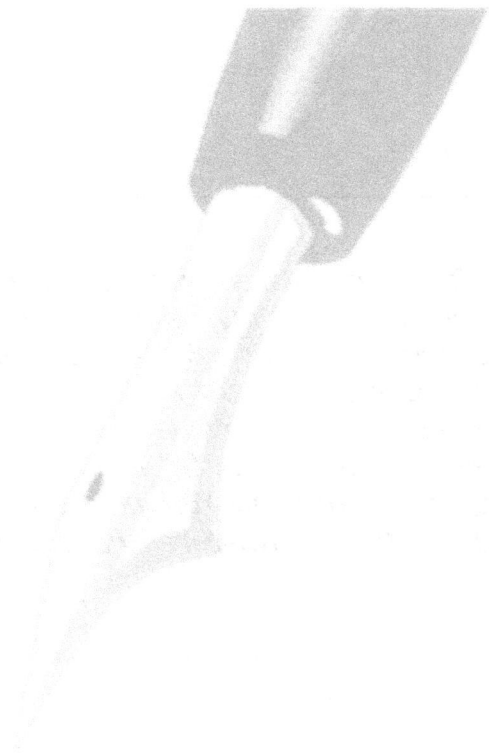

Journal Page ————————————————

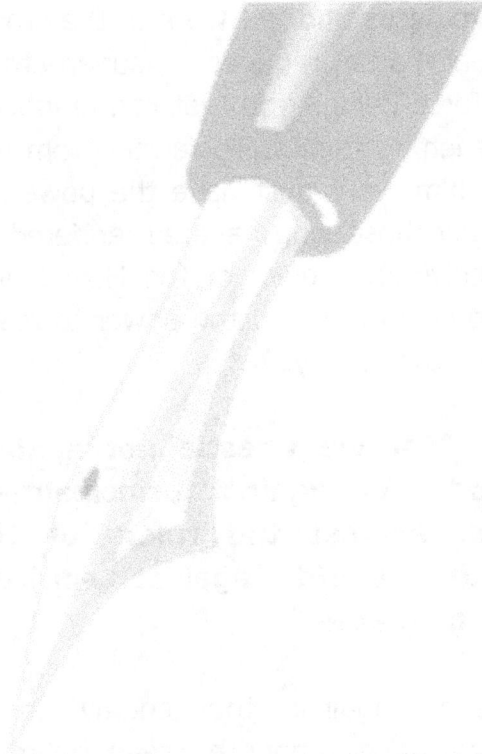

A Spiritual Battle

At the beginning of this journey, I challenged you to surrender to Jesus and the work of the cross. Fighting a spiritual battle requires a supernatural force. There is a force behind you that can empower you to fight the enemy's tactics. To retreat from the enemy and resist him, you must have the power of the Holy Spirit. Only those who have surrendered to Jesus as Lord receive the power of the Holy Spirit. Only submitting to God gives you the power to resist and turn away from the enemy.

Ephesians 6:12 "For we wrestle not against flesh and blood, but against principalities, against powers, against the rulers of the darkness of this world, against spiritual wickedness in high places."

Man wrestles against the enemy in a supernatural realm which cannot be seen by man. Society as a whole is unaware of the battle of darkness in the unseen world. That is why you cannot fight and defeat this enemy on your own natural instincts. Society can see the effects of this battle in the evil and chaos that lurks in the world. One does not have to look far to see the devastation of the evil one. You can read about violent crimes, addictions, corruption, and hate, which are all growing at a fast pace. Yet the common man does not link all this to the unseen enemy who is truly evil and schemes to oppress man. It is the enemy who plants these seeds of wickedness and evil all in a ploy to take man away from God.

The Enemy

The serpent known as the evil one, the devil, and Lucifer, has only one thing in mind after he was cast out of heaven: His aim is to deceive, bringing death and destruction into the lives of man to keep us separated from God. Satan is the liar and the god of adversity. Satan is the enemy of God and man. Lucifer's prime target and goal is to keep man separated from God. God created Lucifer as a beautiful angel. He was so beautiful that he became prideful because of his beauty. Lucifer wanted to be above God, and because of his pride, God cast Lucifer out of the heavens.

Isaiah 14:12-14 "(12) How art thou fallen from heaven, O Lucifer, son of the morning! How art thou cut down to the ground, which didst weaken the nations! (13) For thou hast said in thine heart, I will ascend into heaven, I will exalt my throne above the stars of God: I will sit also upon the mount of the congregation, in the sides of the north: (14) I will ascend above the heights of the clouds; I will be like the most High."

1) From where did Lucifer fall?

2) To where was Lucifer sent?

3) What are the four "I Wills" that Lucifer declared?

Lucifer's pride caused him to be cast out from heaven.

Ezekiel 28:17 "Thine heart was lifted up because of thy beauty, thou hast corrupted thy wisdom by reason of thy brightness: I will cast thee to the ground, I will lay thee before kings, that they may behold thee.
If Lucifer was cast to the ground, where is that location of the ground?"
Job 1:6-7 "(6) Now there was a day when the sons of God came to present themselves before the Lord, and Satan came also among them. (7) And the Lord said unto Satan, Whence comest thou? Then Satan answered the Lord, and said, "from going to and fro in the earth, and from walking up and down in it."

4) What question did the Lord ask Satan?

5) What reply did Satan give the Lord?

1 Peter 5:8 "Be sober, be vigilant; because your adversary the devil, as a roaring lion, walketh about, seeking whom he may devour."

Lucifer has been cast from the heavens to roam the earth's dominion. He walks the earth with a clear mission: to destroy.

6) Define *adversary*.

7) According to 1 Peter, who is the devil's adversary?

8) What is your adversary trying to do?

9) Define the term *devour.*

Man has a spiritual enemy. Man cannot see him, yet he truly exists. This enemy seeks to crush, kill, and destroy man; devouring him, leaving him with no hope. God wants man to be reunited in fellowship with Him and to provide man with peace and a purpose. The enemy, man's opponent, strives to bring darkness and division between God and man.

Satan plans his next move kind of like playing a game of chess. Satan tempts, persuades, and makes his move to destroy. He then sits and watches for your move. Will you approach him and take the bait? Your action, or lack thereof, will provide the strategy for Satan's next move to damage your life. If you start to believe his lies and act in accordance with his plan, you fall farther into the deception of the enemy's snare. Soon the enemy will declare checkmate.

James 4:7 "Submit yourselves therefore to God. Resist the devil, and he will flee from you."

Journal Page _____

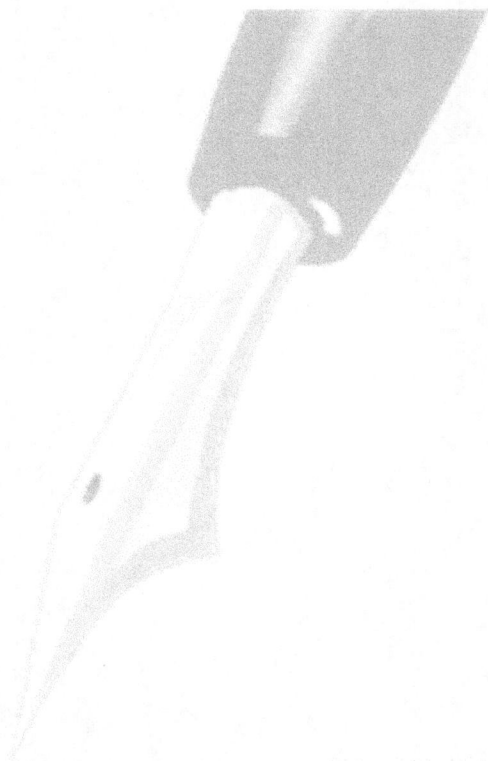

The Power Source

When one surrenders to the power of the cross and to the Lordship of Jesus Christ, ownership of your life also changes. You once were separated from God. While you were apart, the enemy had you in his grasp. The moment you confessed Jesus as your Lord, your life transferred into the hands of God. You are now a child of God! Every child has a birth certificate to prove who her biological parents are, and you have been given a certificate of proof. The proof that you belong to God the Father is the seal of the Holy Spirit. The Holy Spirit dwells inside of you. The Holy Spirit is God's seal—His way of proving that you are His child.

Ephesians 1:13 "In whom ye also trusted, after that ye heard the word of truth, the gospel of your salvation: in whom also after that ye believed, ye were sealed with that Holy Spirit of promise."

You have been sealed. With this seal of God's own Spirit, He has empowered you to move mountains in the name of Jesus. The one who lives in you (the Holy Spirit) is greater than the one in the world (Satan)!

1 John 4:4 "Ye are of God, little children, and have overcome them: because greater is he that is in you, than he that is in the world."

Luke 10:19-20 " (19) Behold, I give unto you power to tread on serpents and scorpions, and over all the power of the enemy: and nothing shall by any means hurt you. (20) Notwithstanding in this rejoice not, that the spirits are subject unto you; but rather rejoice, because your names are written in heaven."

1 Corinthians 6:19 "What know ye not that your body is the temple of the Holy Ghost which is in you, which ye have of God, and ye are not your own?"

John 14:26-27 "(26) But the Comforter, which is the Holy Ghost, whom the Father will send in my name, he shall teach you all things, and bring all things to your remembrance, whatsoever I have said unto you. (27) Peace I leave with you, my peace I give unto you: not as the world giveth, give I unto you. Let not your heart be troubled, neither let it be afraid."

Remember to utilize the journaling pages to record thoughts, answers, and prayers as you continue on this journey!

10) In Ephesians, with what have you been sealed?

11) According to 1 John, who is greater? And, in your own words, what does that mean?

12) In Luke 10, something of great value has been given to you. What is this treasure and what can you do with it?

13) According to John 14, what will the Holy Ghost (Spirit) do for you? Also, what does Jesus tell you in verse 27?

Your power source to declare victory resides in you because it lies in the power of the Holy Spirit dwelling within your heart. Every believer is sealed with the power of the Holy Spirit. Unfortunately, many believers neglect to connect and utilize the power which has been given to them. Experiencing defeat in life is the cause of not connecting correctly with the power and understanding of the Holy Spirit. You need to understand fully who the Spirit is, how He operates, and how you plug into His power to receive power. Many believers never fully plug into the power that is right there for them to have victory.

For example: There is a brand-new lamp on a table. You also have put a brand-new light bulb in the lamp. The lamp is ready, but it is not generating light yet. The lamp cannot light on its own. Your home has an electrical current running through it. You have all the ingredients for the light to have power for lighting, but still it will not light. Why? You must take the cord and plug it into the current of electricity.

It is the same with the power of the Holy Spirit. You must first understand who the Spirit is. You must understand how the Spirit operates. Then you must plug into the source of the power. The Holy

Spirit operates in a supernatural dimension. You live in a natural dimension. It is vital to understand His authority in order to act upon His power and transfer the power into your life. Only the Spirit can battle the defeat in your life. As we said before, the battle is in an unseen world.

➢ LIFE CHANGER #3

1) Do an in-depth Biblical study on the Holy Spirit. Journal your findings.

2) This next exercise may or may not be comfortable for you. In your area, search for a reputable church that actively practices the manifestations of the Spirit. This would be a church that speaks in tongues, slays in the Spirit, and communicates prophetic words. This is what one may call a full gospel or charismatic church, but it is a church that fully moves in the Spirit. Attend with an open mind for what you will see. Attend this church three times.

3) After attending three times, compare your Biblical study with your experience at the church.

4) Continue to seek the understanding of the Spirit.

Without understanding the Spirit's personality, it is very easy to put the Spirit in a box. People try to understand the way God works by a natural understanding, but God is supernatural—so His Spirit works and operates in the supernatural realm. If you do not believe the Spirit's power in the supernatural realm, defeat will often stay at the door of your being.

Zechariah 4:6 Then he answered and spake unto me, saying, "This is the word of the Lord unto Zerubbabel, saying, Not by might, nor by power, but by my spirit, saith the Lord of hosts."

The defeat and battle in your life cannot be won on your own natural ability. Nothing you can do will move the mountain. You cannot use your own power or strength. Victory only comes by the supernatural power and might of the Holy Spirit.

Prayer

Lord, open my eyes to the tactics of the enemy, Satan. Help me to discern the lies and deception that he tries to speak into my life. Illuminate the power of the Holy Spirit in my life. Teach me who the Spirit is and help me to live in the power of the Spirit. God, bring me new revelations of who You are. The victory I seek is found when I live by Your Word and Your power fills me with Your Spirit. Overflow my being with Your Spirit—fill me now! Thank you!

In Jesus' Name,

Amen

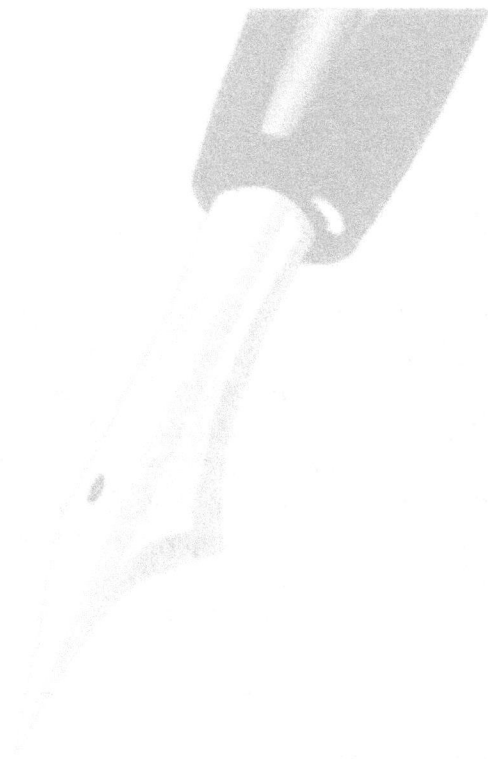

Healing and change in any difficult situation requires three specific actions:

1) Admitting you need help.
2) Reaching out for the help you need.
3) Doing whatever it takes to overcome defeat.

You obviously have already completed Step 1, or this book would not be in your hands. The other two: reaching out for help, and doing whatever it takes, are the most difficult. Reaching out to others is difficult because then it expresses that we need others in our lives.   Depending on the situation, reaching out may be more difficult for some rather than others. The last action: doing whatever it takes is the most difficult of the three. A person will proceed to heal as long as it neither hurts too bad, nor causes too much work to accomplish. The defeat, when not overcome, usually occurs because one wants a quick fix-it solution. Overcoming defeat takes time, hard work, sacrifice, discipline, a deep relationship with Jesus Christ, and an understanding of the Word of God. So before you proceed any further, here is the million dollar question: *"Are you ready to do whatever it takes to prevail?"* If you cannot say with certainty, *"Yes I am,"* then stop right here because I guarantee you this won't be a walk in the park.

For each person, the defeat in his or her life is defined differently. For one it may be low self-esteem; for another, addiction; for another, years of abuse. The tactics the enemy uses to destroy lives are endless. His list of strategies to declare war upon the human race is enormous, and he never gives up waging war.

Exposing the tactic the enemy is using to defeat you opens you to a few issues:

1) Exposing the tactic declares war on the enemy. War indicates that there is a battle, so this means the enemy will work harder to discourage you. Understand that even when things get tough, God is still working.

2) Depending upon your battle, exposing your struggle opens vulnerability in your life. As you continue to peel back the layers of what is actually defeating you, it can open old scars of fear, pain, guilt, and shame. These emotions are also used to keep you captive to your defeat. Because these emotions are difficult to hit head on and they seem easier to keep hidden and quiet, people usually choose to live in the realm of defeat, rather than to open the scars.

You can break the chains and begin living beyond defeat. It starts with an "I will" statement. *I will choose life and blessing.*

Deuteronomy 30:19-20 "(19) I call heaven and earth to record this day against you, that I have set before you life and death, blessing and

cursing: therefore choose life, that both thou and thy seed may live: (20) That thou mayest love the Lord thy God, and that thou mayest obey his voice, and that thou mayest cleave unto him: for he is thy life, and the length of thy days: that thou mayest dwell in the land which the Lord sware unto thy fathers, to Abraham, to Isaac, and to Jacob, to give them."

1) What has God set before you that you may choose?

2) In verse 20, what three things must you do to choose life and blessing?

3) Define *cleave* as used in verse 20.

4) Once you have defined *cleave*, in your own words, how does that relate to God, your relationship with him, and what you are experiencing as defeat?

Sign your own contract:

I (your name) _____choose this day (date)
_____, life and blessing. I will do whatever
it takes, even when it gets difficult to capture victory
and freedom. If I do not march into victory, then I
know it is because I did not do what was needed to
claim Christ's victory as mine.

Signature:

_____

It is time to begin to expose your defeat. You
cannot move forward until you define the battle that
you are up against. Exposing defeat is about declaring
emotions, people, or circumstances that ignite the
attitude of negative defeat.

➢ **LIFE CHANGER #4**

On the journaling pages, write in detail your testimony of defeat that you are battling. A testimony is simply your own life story, in this case, as it pertains to your struggles with defeat. Include in this testimony details of the following:

1) Emotions that are triggered, involving people and/or circumstances.

2) Where the defeat seemed to begin, as well as its present state.

3) Steps you have taken (if any) to rise above this defeat, OR Why you have not taken any steps.

4) If you have taken steps to overcome, what caused these steps to fail?

5) Review your testimony.

6) Underline all the people involved—yourself included—in your testimony. Write beside each name any emotions or thoughts about that individual.

7) Highlight times you used words that pertain to yourself like *I, me, mine,* or *myself.*

As you look over all you have done, prayerfully ask God to reveal to you what is defeating you. As you review and pray over this testimony, God may reveal multiple areas in your life that are defeat-oriented. For example, let's say you initially believed you were only struggling with healing a broken relationship. As you write and review your testimony, God may reveal where you are not willing to forgive someone, or reveal a bigger issue of mistrust in your life. The testimony you have written is to detail and define the whole problem, not just scratch the surface. Many times the issue of defeat has many areas that need to be addressed. To define what the struggle is in-depth breaks all the chains to be set free and walk in victory.

The list you have written may appear overwhelming, but take heart! Do not look at the entire list at once. This is where you must determine if medical professionals, counseling assistance, or other programs must assist you. Refer back to the beginning of the book and review the list. This book is to lead you into a relationship with God and a lifestyle of depending on His Word and power. God is all-powerful, but He has sent people in this world who are specifically designed to give professional help in serious situations. This book alone is not a substitute for professional help when addressing deeper-rooted issues.

If you are in need of professional assistance, stop now and seek that help!

As you look over your list, write down your hopes for what you've listed and then clear goals for your life change. Write in-depth descriptions of what victory, freedom, and peace look like to you.

Hebrews 11:1 "Now faith is the substance of things hoped for, the evidence of things not seen."

The process of this life change can be difficult. Earlier I wrote that when fear, pain, and difficulty set in, this is when one gives up and does not do what it takes to overcome. It will get difficult. When it gets difficult, I want you to read what you wrote about your goals for victory. This will renew your hope and strength and help you keep your eyes on the prize. As life change occurs and chains begin to break, the enemy will attack. He will pierce into your heart to discourage and try to rob you of hope and progress. What does the above verse tell you about faith? It is the substance of things hoped for but not yet seen. Faith is simply saying: *I have victory and this is what I hope for, even though I cannot see it yet. I know it will happen—I will have victory.* If you read your victory statement and believe what it says and not what is happening in the moment, this will give you courage to get back up and fight some more.

Philippians 1:6 "Being confident of this very thing, that he which hath begun a good work in you will perform it until the day of Jesus Christ"

Philippians 4:13 "I can do all things through Christ which strengtheneth me."

On individual index cards or sticky notes, write out Hebrews 11:1, Philippians 1:6, and Philippians 4:13. Place them in areas that you can read them each day, like your bathroom mirror, car dashboard, or office cubicle. Begin to memorize these scriptures to add to your strength.

1) What is faith? (Hebrews 11:1)

2) If you cannot see faith, how do you hold onto it?

3) In what can you be confident? (Philippians 1:6)

4) Who is doing and finishing the work?

5) How many things can you do according to Philippians 4:13, and who gives you the strength?

Prayer

Lord, you have begun the work to lead me into the glory of victory. Help me to keep my eyes on the prize of my hope for victory. Lord, help me to remember that You will never leave my side. Reveal to me all that I am holding onto that leads to defeat. Today I choose life and blessing. Help me to find the path to that blessing. Help me in Your strength to do whatever it takes to claim victory in the name of Jesus Christ, my Lord.

In Jesus' Name, _____

Amen

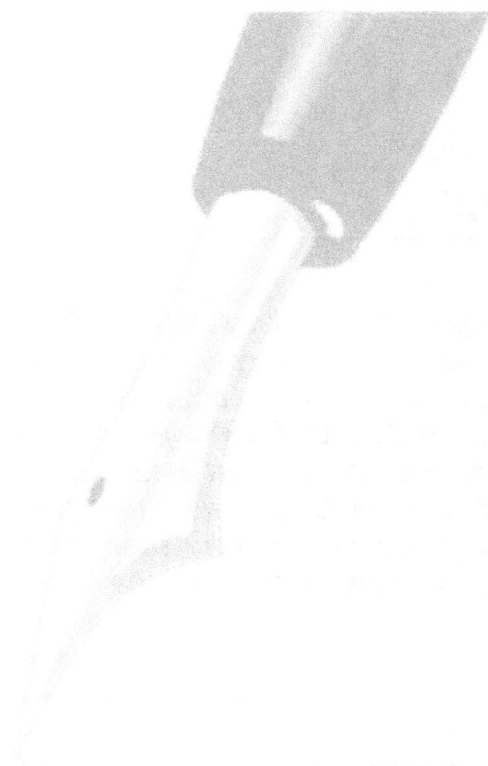

OWNING YOUR PROBLEM

The first difficult task to hurdle is to take ownership of your problem. As you read your testimony, ask yourself, *whose testimony was it?* You need to come to terms with the realization that it is *your* testimony. As you read your testimony, who is experiencing the struggle? *You* are. As you read your testimony, who is taking negative action, or feeling negative emotions, or behaving in a manner that is not acceptable? *You* are. Who is the one being affected by whatever you wrote in the testimony? *You are experiencing the defeat in your life.*

Yes, it is true that maybe others have behaved badly and possibly imposed upon you certain unacceptable actions. Some struggles may have simply been circumstances that life just dumped on you, a sour deal. There is a wide range of scenarios that bring a whirlwind of defeat, but there is one universal connection with all defeat. For everyone who experiences defeat, they choose to allow people or circumstances to keep them defeated. The defeat is affecting your emotions, your actions, your thoughts and habits, or lack thereof. The defeat is holding you back from becoming all that God wants you to be. You are allowing the defeat to define your attitude rather than allowing God to walk you through the difficulty and walking you into victory.

It is time to stop blaming and making excuses for why you are experiencing defeat. Others may have had a hand in creating a circumstance—for instance, someone could have betrayed you. Betrayal certainly hurts and disrupts your life, but you cannot let it defeat you. The next step is where *you* take the responsibility. How did you respond to the betrayal? You and only you can determine how you will react to the first blow. How did you work through your emotions? You can choose to harbor hate and bitterness, or you can choose to heal using positive action. What you choose to do at this point is your responsibility. You made choices which brought you to this place of defeat. You cannot change others; you can only control your own reactions. Circumstances and people may not change. They may not even want to change; but your heart, your attitude, your actions *can* change. You are the deciding factor that determines what you want to hold on to and what you are willing to release.

I have someone who will always be a part of my life, until death we do part. This person has always gone out of his way to harm me. He would accuse me falsely, he would try to get me fired from my job, and these are only a few things that took place. With each vicious blow I would get angrier and build more bitterness against this person. I couldn't even hear his name without knots turning in my stomach. I would not go anywhere he would be present. I let what he had done to me run in my mind like a recorder. I would dwell on what he was going to do next. As I thought of past and present issues that occurred, I would get angry, and then I would want to get even. I allowed his actions to determine my thoughts and behavior. I chose to act on those emotions by separating myself from fun activities because he was there. I blamed what he did to me for my bitterness, anger, and having to exclude myself from activities because I couldn't be around him. The truth is he didn't keep me from activities. He didn't plant in my head to get angry or to harbor bitterness. He didn't say, "Don't forgive me!" I chose every step of the way to do all those things. I allowed him to have control over my emotions, my will, and my choices. I had to choose to own and take responsibility for the fact that I was dwelling on anger, bitterness, and excluding myself. Therefore I had to make a decision: just as I chose to live negatively, I needed to choose to live positively. I had to choose to forgive and release what he had done and not allow it to control me any longer.

You must do the same. Someone or something may have ignited the first spark, but you made the fire flame. Today you must choose to no longer blame others or circumstances for your defeat. You have the power over your actions, your thoughts, and how you choose to deal with life. You have the victory—you just have not made the choice to take the right path.

➢ LIFE CHANGER #5

Review your testimony once again. Journal about why you are responsible for your own actions and emotions. In your own words, state why these actions and emotions are *your* problem and only yours. Also, write how you need to reverse your actions or thoughts to make positive choices about the circumstances or people involved.

Prayer

Lord, forgive me for blaming others for the emotions and actions in my life. I have chosen to allow these emotions and actions to become a major, negative aspect of my life. Help me to pull these emotions out and transform them into Your truth. Heal my life: take my stony, hard heart and replace it with Your compassionate spirit. Thank you!

In Jesus' Name,   _____

Amen

Journal Page ───────────────

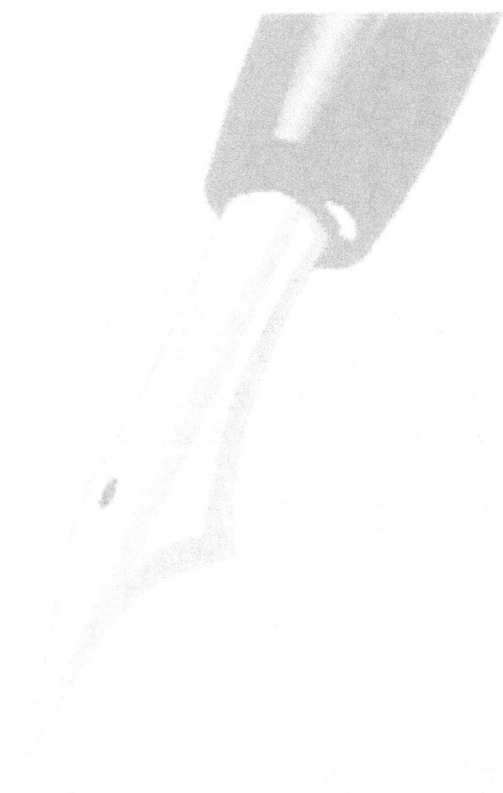

Journal Page ——————————————

Transformation

Romans 12:2 "And be not conformed to this world: but be ye transformed by the renewing of your mind, that ye may prove what is that good, and acceptable, and perfect, will of God."

1) Define the following words:
   Transform
   Renew

Transformation is vital to move from defeat into victory. The Word of God transforms your way of thinking, which then in turn changes your way of action. This transformation then changes your whole lifestyle, including habits, thoughts, and actions. Transformation is exchanging lies for God's truth. Transformation is taking the defeat the enemy has planted in your life and replacing that defeat with the power of God's truth. Transformation states: *I will change who I am according to the Word of God.*

You are dealing with fears, thoughts, habits, hurts, and actions that are called *strongholds*. They are called this because they are doing just that: they are strongly holding onto you. These strongholds keep you captive to the defeat you are experiencing. Take a moment right now and reread your testimony. Find thoughts, hurts, and actions that hold you in bondage to that defeat. Those are your strongholds that must be broken and torn down. Transformation will take place when you renew your mind with the Word of God. The Word of God breaks those strongholds. The Word of God is your weapon in this war of defeat.

If you are to bring down the strongholds you must bring every negative thought, action, and belief into captivity and exchange those thoughts, beliefs, and actions under the obedience of Christ. Now is the time to bring down the strongholds.

2 Corinthians 10:4-5 "(4) For the weapons of our warfare are not carnal, but mighty through God to the pulling down of strong holds; (5) Casting down imaginations, and every high thing that exalteth itself against the knowledge of God, and bringing into captivity every thought to the obedience of Christ"

➢ **LIFE CHANGER #6**

This life changer will take quite some time—be patient!

So far you should have completed a detailed testimony. Details include your emotions, thoughts, actions and complete dialogue of your struggle. Through the process of dissecting your testimony, you have determined to the best of your knowledge what has held you in captivity to the bondage of defeat. This includes people, emotions, actions, choices, circumstances, and all else that is involved. With this on your mind, proceed with the following:

1) Combine your notes into one complete list of what you believe are strongholds that keep you in the bondage of defeat.

2) Choose four issues that you believe are priorities—in the most desperate need of transformation.

3) Write each word or phrase that labels that issue on an index card. For example, if you believe it is anger, write down *anger*. You will use a separate index card for each issue.

4) Search for two scriptures for each issue that attack that struggle with God's truth. Add them to your index cards. For example: If you are angry, find two scripture passages that instruct on what to do with that anger.

5) Begin memorizing those scriptures. In fact, carry those scriptures (on the index cards) with you. When the enemy starts igniting those negative actions, emotions, or thoughts, pull out the scriptures and immediately meditate on them.

Memorizing scripture transfers truth from your head to your heart. Memorizing scripture also helps you pull it out anywhere you are, no matter what you are doing, because it is in your memory. It becomes a part of you forever.

Psalm 119:11 "Thy word have I hid in mine heart, that I might not sin against thee."

When you have memorized scriptures and transformed your mind—meaning God has helped you master and win captive those emotions, thoughts, and actions so that those strongholds no longer hold you captive—continue to do the same with the rest of your list of struggles until they are completed and transformed.

While you're working toward memorization and transformation, now would be a perfect time to start disciplining yourself to read a chapter of the Bible a day. Find a quiet place where you will not be distracted. Journal what the Word reveals to you. Start with the New Testament and refresh yourself with the stories of Jesus.

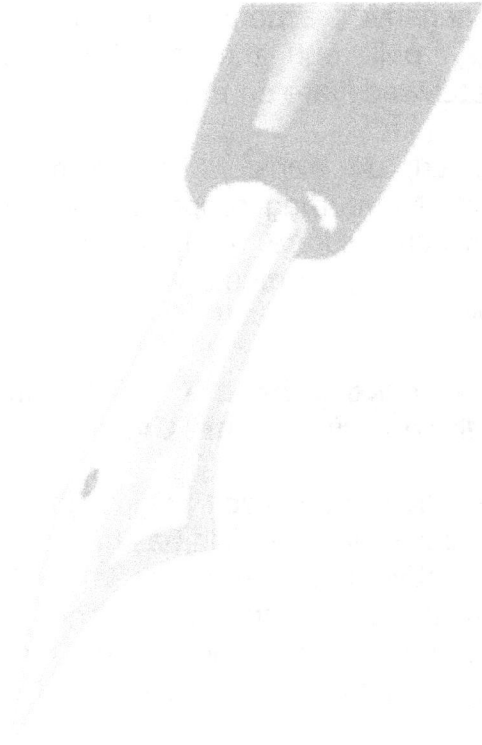

➤ LIFE CHANGER: UPDATE

First Half of the Journey

At this point of the book you should have completed the following life changes:

1) Surrender to Jesus
2) Attend church weekly
3) Biblical study on the Holy Spirit
4) Attend a full gospel church at least three times
5) Compare your study with your experience
6) Write your testimony of defeat
7) Define your defeat and pray over that definition
8) Make a list combining all the issues that hold you captive to defeat
9) Choose and write on index cards your top four issues
10) Find two scriptures to exchange those issues for truth, and begin memorizing them
11) Read one chapter of the Bible each day

Prayer

Lord, thank you for your Word. Teach me, correct me, and direct me with Your written Word. Help me to transform my negative thoughts according the truth of Your Word. I want to exchange all the lies in my heart and renew and replace them with the truth of the Spirit. Hide scripture in my heart so that I may not sin against You.

In Jesus' Name, _____

Amen

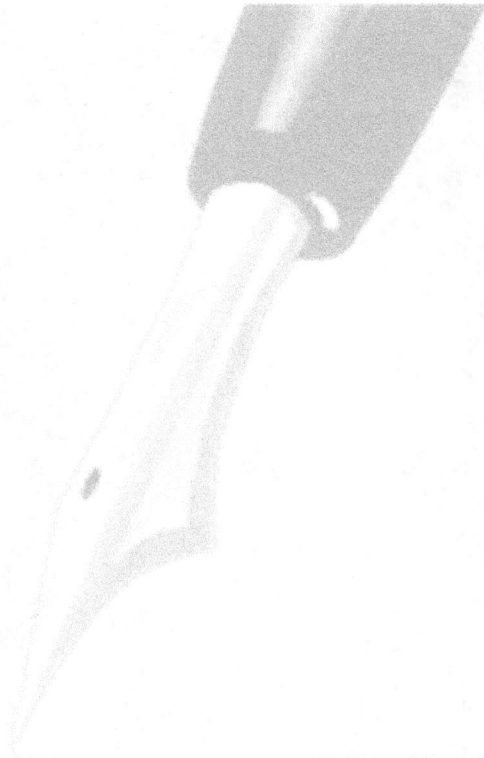

Releasing the Defeat ──────────────

How many people know your entire struggle in-depth? Do they know your deepest pain? Do they know your fears? Do they know your thoughts or actions? Do they know your weaknesses?

One of the tactics Satan uses to orchestrate a plan to keep you in bondage is to captivate your thoughts and silence them. If Satan can keep you silent, then he can pour lies into your mind and dance in your head. Satan used this tactic on me, and I fell into the trap of silence. With all the choices and problems of my family, the enemy shackled me. He would speak lies in my head such as: *You can't tell anyone—how would that look—you are a leader of the church and you can't even take care of your own family!* He would also accuse me of being a terrible parent and I thought that if I spoke to anyone, they would not only judge me, but my children too. Soon I became shackled to guilt and shame. As Satan continued to speak in my head, I would keep even more silent regarding the circumstances in our lives. I secluded myself so that no one could really find out about all of the defeat that I was feeling. Some people knew bits and pieces, but the parts of the stories I never shared, such as my fears, or my mistakes—that is where the enemy hit the bull's-eye. That was his point of attack when I kept my struggles silent.

James 5:16 "Confess your faults one to another, and pray one for another, that ye may

be healed. The effectual fervent prayer of a righteous man availeth much."

1 John 1:9 "If we confess our sins, he is faithful and just to forgive us our sins, and to cleanse us from all unrighteousness."

James 5:13-16 "(13) Is any among you afflicted? let him pray. Is any merry? let him sing psalms.(14) Is any sick among you? let him call for the elders of the church; and let them pray over him, anointing him with oil in the name of the Lord: (15) And the prayer of faith shall save the sick, and the Lord shall raise him up; and if he have committed sins, they shall be forgiven him. (16) Confess your faults one to another, and pray one for another, that ye may be healed. The effectual fervent prayer of a righteous man availeth much."

Galatians 6:2 "Bear ye one another's burdens, and so fulfil the law of Christ."

1 Thessalonians 5:11 "Wherefore comfort yourselves together, and edify one another, even as also ye do."

    1) What are you to confess? (James 5:16)

    2) What happens when you confess your sins? (1 John 1:9)

    3) In your own words, explain James 5:13-16.

4) According to Galatians, what are we to bear?

5) In 1 Thessalonians 5:11, what have we been commanded to do for one another?

You are told the importance of sharing your sins, your thoughts, your adversities, and releasing those things into the hands of other believers. Releasing your burdens and being accountable to others for all these things brings healing and restoration in a diversity of ways. Confessing releases the guilt that could be lurking in your heart. When you share all things, you are accepting responsibility for that which you are responsible for and releasing not only guilt, but also the oppressing shame. Sharing allows others to pray and fight on your behalf. Sharing brings others alongside you to comfort and encourage through the difficult times. Sharing releases the prideful thought that you are capable of doing it on your own. When you share, what you are really doing is building yourself an army to attack Satan and to reverse his tactics of defeat. Believers will stand with you. Remember the object lesson of the three-strand cord! Strength comes in numbers! Releasing provides the protection, transformation, and healing that is much needed for victory. When you bring others into your territory to surround you, the burden is then carried together. Everyone needs a cheerleader to cheer them on. Look at other believers as the cheerleaders to encourage you on to victory!

➢ LIFE CHANGER #7

I hope that you have been attending a church of your own choosing weekly. Church is a great place to begin connecting not only with God, but also with other believers who can surround you in times of struggle as well as joy. Your next life-changing experience is to connect with a small group of believers with whom you can intimately share your struggles. This small group may be a Sunday School class, a mid-week Bible study, or even a Biblically-based group outside of church that deals with your specific need.

These smaller groups are designed for intimate, more closely-related relationships. As you start attending regularly, you will begin building trust and friendships at a different level. As you build the relationships, start sharing as much as you feel comfortable. As time goes by, the goal is to share all that you are battling. This sharing is not so the group will fix the problem. Instead, remember that sharing your struggles can provide:

- Releasing thoughts so the enemy cannot keep you captive to those thoughts.
- Others to fight the battle alongside of you.
- Building a team for support.
- Prayer covering from others.
- Encouragement from others.
- Others helping you carry the burden, making it lighter.
- Healing and transformation.

- New, deeper friendships that believe as you do.

As you continue to grow in relationship with this group, you will begin to feel a sense of freedom. God did not design us to struggle without the relationship of other believers. The enemy will try to isolate you. Isolation is the tactic of Satan to hold captive the entire scenario. Release the burdens—do not be afraid.

Prayer

Lord, lead me to the group of people that will allow me to trust. Help me to have the courage and strength to release my difficulties into the hands of others. God, break the chains of silence in my life. Help me not to fear, but to instead place my fear in Your hands. I cannot do this on my own. I need other believers and Your Holy Spirit to walk with me during this time.

In Jesus' Name,   _____

Amen

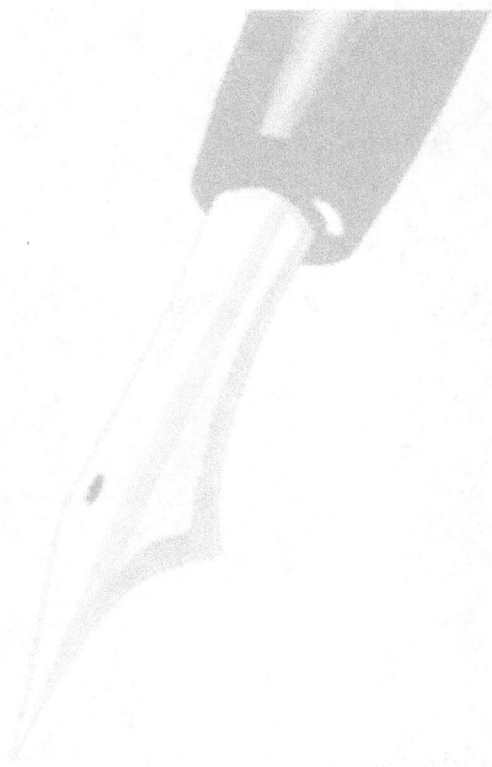

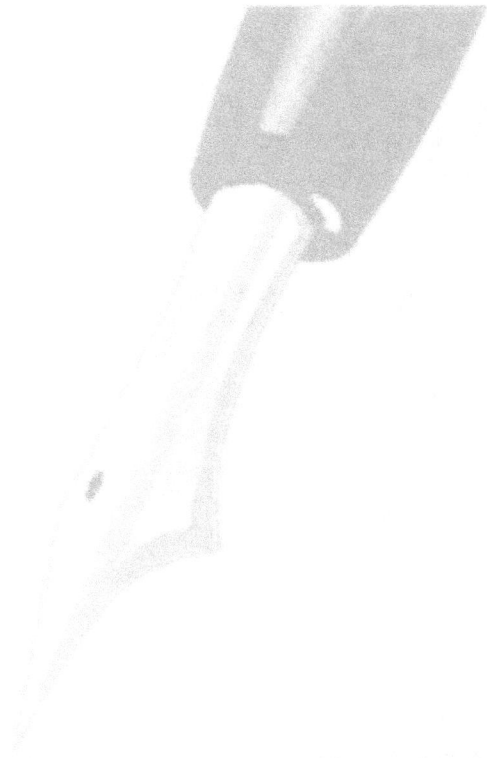

Journal Page

Forgiving Yourself

Life will throw a number of adversities in your path. Scattered across this road you travel are all sizes and shapes of hurdles that you may encounter. These hurdles are big players in keeping you chained to defeat. The three biggest hurdles that are often difficult to jump are: forgiving yourself, forgiving others, and holding on to anger. When you cannot find rest in these three areas, often the effects of shame and guilt start to creep their way in to choke you.

As you wrote about the difficulties of your adversity and the emotions, people, and the details of the adversity, what surfaced? Did the testimony expose any self-inflicting pain such as actions that you carried out that were less than acceptable? Did any regrets of *should have, could have,* or *would have,* appear? Did you carry out any actions against others that you were regretful about and wished that you could just re-do it all? When this kind of deep examination of one's self is exposed, it is often difficult to forgive your actions. This heaps mounds of guilt on your heart.

1 John 1:9 "If we confess our sins, he is faithful and just to forgive us our sins, and to cleanse us from all unrighteousness."

Matthew 6:12 "And forgive us our debts, as we forgive our debtors."

Acts 26:18 "To open their eyes, and to turn them from darkness to light, and from the power of Satan unto God, that they may receive forgiveness of sins, and inheritance among them which are sanctified by faith that is in me."

Isaiah 43:25 "I, even I, am he that blotteth out thy transgressions for mine own sake, and will not remember thy sins."

Colossians 2:14 "Blotting out the handwriting of ordinances that was against us, which was contrary to us, and took it out of the way, nailing it to his cross"

1) According to 1 John, if we confess our sin, what happens?

2) In Isaiah, what is blotted out and never remembered again?

3) According to Colossians, if you confessed, what happened to the ordinances against you?

Shame and Guilt

Shame and guilt are tactics that Satan uses to infuse together all the areas where you may have fallen short of positive choices. For example, with my children, when they made life choices that were negative, Satan would plant a seed in my thoughts to make me believe that my lack of parenting was the cause of their actions. When I started to believe those lies, I felt guilty and carried their choices as if I had chosen for them. I started blaming my lack of discipline or direction as the cause of their chosen actions. Shame can begin to root when you are too embarrassed to expose actions that you have taken. Dan and I declared bankruptcy due to our overspending. Once that bankruptcy was final I was ashamed of those actions because I knew we were wrong, but still chose to take that course of action.

As you read earlier in a scripture in Romans, all people fall short of the glory of God. You also have read many scriptures thus far on sin and forgiveness. The point I am trying to make is simply this: You should never discard the negative choices or actions you commit. You should remember that *all* people fall short in one way or another. No one is perfect, they may just hide it better. The good news is this: Jesus died for all that guilt and shame, for all that sin and wrong so that you would have another chance to choose right and truth.

Shame and guilt are highly related to forgiving yourself. Harboring shame and guilt happens when we cannot forgive ourselves for something we did, or failed to do. So let's make a life change and begin to forgive yourself for anything—even something that you feel is too difficult to forgive.

➢ **LIFE CHANGER #8**

The first step to forgiving yourself is to simply confess that you acted or did something that was wrong. If your heart is filled with pain—and you feel repentant—then cry out to Jesus to forgive you of that pain you caused and you will be forgiven.

1) Write down what you have done for which you need forgiveness. Include specifics like what occurred, your actions, thoughts, etc.

2) Write a heart-felt confession of forgiveness for the wrong that you have committed. Pray over this confession.

3) It is done! You may not feel differently, but re-read the previous scriptures—what do they say about those sins that you have committed and confessed?

Isaiah 1:18 "Come now, and let us reason together, saith the Lord: though your sins be as scarlet, they shall be as white as snow; though they be red like crimson, they shall be as wool."

Your sins: they are washed away, white and clean. By the death of Jesus on the cross, you have been forgiven!

There is one more step that is vital for healing. As you listed the wrongs of your circumstance, did you hurt or wrong anyone else in the process? Part of healing and forgiving yourself often involves making wrongs into rights. We call that restitution. Ask God in prayer how others may have been affected by your wrongdoing. Ask God to reveal to you how this wrong you imposed upon this person may have hurt them and what you may need to do, if anything, to heal the situation. For example, if you said hurtful words out of anger to another person, God may have you return to that individual to apologize and heal the relationship. Once you have established that an action is required, go back to that person to take accountability for your hurtful actions. Prayerfully choose the words and how you will approach this specific area.

There is no room for defending your emotions. You are giving up all rights to what led up to your negative actions. The sole purpose of returning to heal what you had done is simply to take accountability for your action. You should not expect a certain outcome. The only purpose for returning and apologizing is simply to make things right in your life. Understand that the action you inflicted may have done irreversible damage. You may apologize and take full responsibility for your actions, but the receiver of that apology may not accept your words or intent. The purpose of this retribution is a healing process for you. Releasing and admitting your wrong, then returning to take responsibility for it, is all done so the one you mistreated is recognized, and you have owned that mistake. To face the one you have wronged and to humbly admit and take full responsibility is never an easy task. Doing this helps to bring the forgiveness you need to heal and it breaks the cycle of the ugly chain we call shame.

Remember that shame and guilt are self-abusive tactics to eat and decay your soul.

Depending upon the actions you have committed, forgiving yourself may take many times of reading those scriptures and transforming your mind to believe you are forgiven. Every time Satan wants to throw the arrow at you to make you think you can never be forgiven, take out the sword of the Spirit (which is the Word of God, the Holy Scripture, the Bible) and say: *I am forgiven. The Word of God confirms it and I believe it! I am forgiven.* You are forgiven!

Prayer

Lord, help me to understand that you nailed all my sins to the cross, and cast them as far as the east is from the west. In doing so, you remember them no more. Hallelujah! Although my sins are red as scarlet, you have made them white as snow. Open my heart to forgive myself as you have forgiven me. Help me to move beyond self-condemnation and walk into freedom. Thank you, Jesus for all You've done. I will forgive myself as you have forgiven me.

In Jesus' Name, _____

Amen

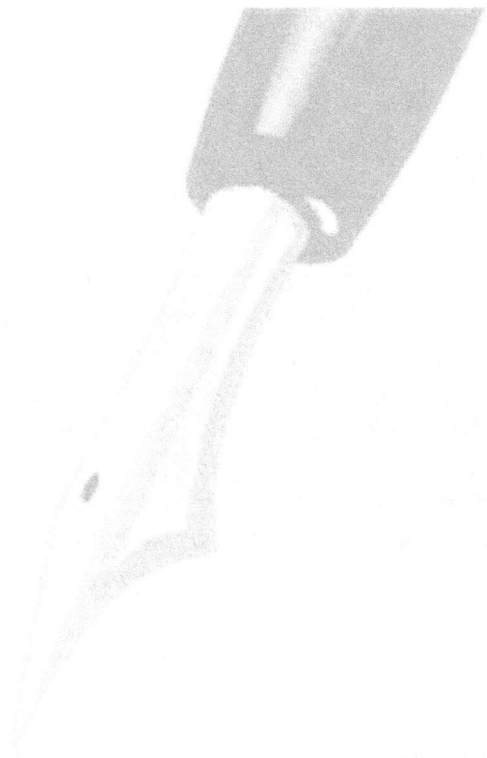

Forgiving Others

      Many times in life we are betrayed and hurt by the actions of others. Often there is no doubt that those offenses were malicious and without care of how their actions may have harmed you. You can justify the reasons to hold on to anger, grudges, and resentment. However, holding on to these emotions harm only one person: you! Holding on to these emotions as they rage in your soul create bitterness, hate, strife, and much more. Little by little, decay begins, eating at your soul, bringing upon you more negative emotions that become deeper-rooted. This decay robs you of joy, peace, and rest. Forgiving others is an antidote for the decay.

      Forgiving someone does not mean that you forget—it means you release them from allowing their actions to hurt you. Forgiving someone does not free *them* of their actions; rather the person it frees is *you*. It is often easier to apologize when you were the offender than to forgive someone of their offense to you. Forgiving someone gives up your right to be hurt by them. Forgiving someone may also mean you need to put boundaries around the friendship. In certain circumstances you may not be able to socialize with or trust this person again. In others, you may be able to continue the friendship at a lower degree of intimacy. In either case, forgiveness is a mandatory action given by God. It is truth that will set you free.

Matthew 18:21-22 "(21) Then came Peter to him, and said, Lord, how oft shall my brother sin against me, and I forgive him? till seven

times? (22) Jesus saith unto him, I say not unto thee, Until seven times: but, Until seventy times seven."

John 8:7 "So when they continued asking him, he lifted up himself, and said unto them, He that is without sin among you, let him first cast a stone at her."

Matthew 7:5 "Thou hypocrite, first cast out the beam out of thine own eye; and then shalt thou see clearly to cast out the mote out of thy brother's eye."

1) How many times does Matthew say to forgive?

2) According to John, are you without fault or sin?

3) In your own words, explain Matthew 7:5.

Forgiving others is a commandment given by God. To forgive others, take a peek inside your own life and actions. Are you without sin? Have you ever had the need for someone to forgive you? When you needed forgiveness, did you hope that they would forgive you for that act? Did Jesus forgive you of any of your sins? Were any of your sins too large for Him to refuse forgiveness?

Love is what drove Jesus to the cross—love for you, even while you were still a sinner. The cross and His love provided forgiveness for *all* sin. The blood of

Jesus on that cross provided forgiveness for the sins of the past, the sins of the present and even future sins. Love demands forgiving others as you have been forgiven. You do not just forgive because if feels good. Forgiving others brings healing and restoration. Love covers a multitude of sins. Forgiving does not just restore and heal those that are forgiven, but it restores and heals your spirit.

When you forgive an individual, you begin to supply an antidote to the poison that Satan's lies have poured into your veins. The Aramaic word for *forgive* means *to untie.* When you really forgive another for the offense that he has imposed upon you, you begin to untie the bitterness and anger that have strangled you for so long. The conscious decision to stop allowing the bitterness, anger, or hurt to strangle you is one that you have to make. Reality is this: you allowed that act to cause you pain, and you nurtured that negativity to feed those emotions. Yes, the act could have been very painful. How you responded to the pain was your choice of action.

How many times have you told the story of how that person hurt you and how the action has affected you? STOP telling the story of hurt. You are feeding into the lies of Satan. Start telling the story of forgiveness.

➢ **LIFE CHANGER #9**

1) Start praying for God to open your heart to forgive that person who has hurt you.

2) Write a letter releasing the wrong that person has done. In this letter, tell the offender that you forgive them, naming specifically the offense. This could be done in your journal; it does not necessarily need to be sent to that person. Remember this forgiveness is for you more than it is for them.

3) Write a prayer asking God to help you release this person into His hands and to show you how to love this person.

4) Pray for the offender at your regular prayer time with God. You will know when you have actually forgiven them when you can hear or say their names without any negative, hurtful thoughts occurring.

Prayer

Lord, my heart is heavy. Please help me to forgive (insert name/names). I don't know where to begin on my own. Show me how to change the pain into healing. I want to forgive (name/names) so that You can begin to help me to heal the scars of the hurt. Lord, I thank you for healing my heart and helping me to forgive.

In Jesus' Name, _____

Amen

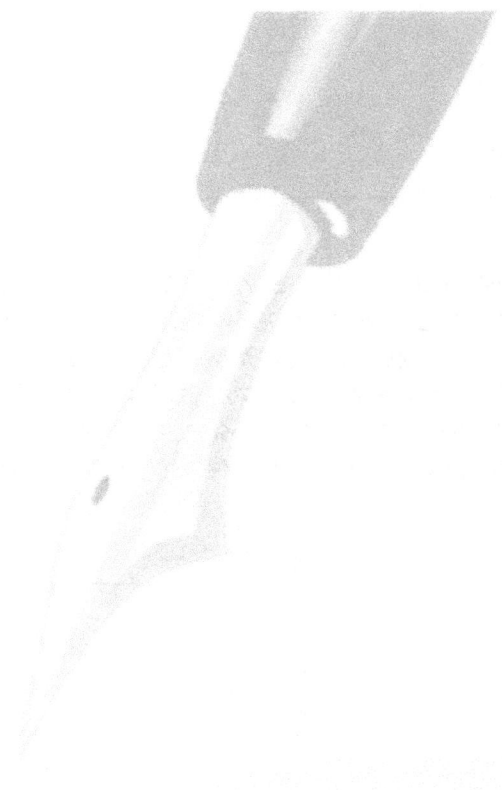

Anger is a *real* emotion. Yes, anger occurs when you have been mistreated or wronged. Anger erupts when one feels that justice was not served. The feeling itself is not the problem; rather, it is often a *good* emotion. The problem occurs when anger arises and you do not deal with the anger in a positive way. How you decide to release this anger dictates if it becomes destructive or not. When anger comes to the forefront of your life, what actions surface? Anger can destroy relationships. If when you are angry, verbal abuse or violent abuse triggers uncontrollably, then I would say you may have destructive anger issues. The anger that is uncontrolled can often create health issues or leave you with a state of mind that is less than stable. Depending on your outbursts of anger and your actions at this point, you may need a professional evaluation to see if you need further assistance. Please seek additional help if necessary.

First let us address this: anger *can be positive.* God gave us the emotion of anger. For example, read the story of Jesus in the temple, found in Mark 11:15-17. Jesus turned over the tables because He was angry over injustice. The people in the temple were taking advantage of others by selling goods dishonestly. You are allowed to be angry at injustice and such things that may occur; however, the emotion you call anger is not the problem. Anger can and should be expressed, but it must be expressed in a manner that is upright and beneficial.

When I suggest that we get rid of anger, I am talking about anger that leads to a deeper bondage of negative consequence. Anger that is controlled gives the Spirit of God the advantage, not the enemy.

Anger can be controlled. You may not be able to control a situation, but you can control how you redirect your anger in a positive manner. Anger is a healthy emotion—to suppress anger is not the antidote. With anger, the goal is to express it in a constructive manner that brings communication. When you allow anger to control your actions, hostility emerges and gives way to urges that may create destruction. This may look like an active rage of breaking and throwing things, it may be a physical attack, or it may even be a self-inflicted harm of some kind.

Psalm 37:8 "Cease from anger, and forsake wrath: fret not thyself in any wise to do evil."

Proverbs 29:22 "An angry man stirreth up strife, and a furious man aboundeth in transgression."

Proverbs 30:33 "Surely the churning of milk bringeth forth butter, and the wringing of the nose bringeth forth blood: so the forcing of wrath bringeth forth strife."

Proverbs 14:29 "He that is slow to wrath is of great understanding: but he that is hasty of spirit exalteth folly."

Proverbs 19:11 "The discretion of a man deferreth his anger; and it is his glory to pass over a transgression."

Ecclesiastes 7:9 "Be not hasty in thy spirit to be angry: for anger resteth in the bosom of fools."

Ephesians 4:26-27 "(26) Be ye angry, and sin not: let not the sun go down upon your wrath: (27) Neither give place to the devil."

Colossians 3:8, 12-13 "(8) But now ye also put off all these; anger, wrath, malice, blasphemy, filthy communication out of your mouth... (12) Put on therefore, as the elect of God, holy and beloved, bowels of mercies, kindness, humbleness of mind, meekness, longsuffering; (13) Forbearing one another, and forgiving one another, if any man have a quarrel against any: even as Christ forgave you, so also do ye."

Anger is a self- absorbed emotion. When anger is making you burst into a volcanic eruption, there is an underlying cause of a hurt or scar that is much larger that the act that had ignited the outburst of anger.

1) According to Psalm 37:8, what should you cease from doing?

2) In Proverbs 29:22, what does a hot-tempered man stir up and cause?

3) Ephesians 4:26-27 cautions that when one is angry, to whom do they give a foothold?

4) According to Colossians what should one get rid of in his life? What should one exchange for anger?

Anger gives Satan a foothold to work in your life. He uses unhealthy anger for his advantage to destroy your health, your state of mind, and ultimately your relationships. Anger expressed in a destructive context creates devastation. It is like a tornado, tearing down everything in its path.

➤ LIFE CHANGER #10

Please Note: If your anger is violent and uncontrollable, seek professional help to manage it. Do not go that path alone.

1) Write about what ignites your anger and how you respond to it.

2) List the negative responses to anger that you have acted out. How does that anger affect you and your relationships with others?

3) Beside the negative responses, write how you can respond in a more positive manner while still expressing what is bothering you.

4) Pray that God will help you control your anger.

5) Start putting the positive responses to action when you feel you are getting angry.

Prayer

Lord, reveal to me where I need to forgive. Help me to not only forgive myself for all that I allow to haunt me, but also help me to forgive (name person or persons who have offended). Help me to love myself and (offender's name). Lord, at times my anger rages destructively. Have the Holy Spirit remind me to not give the devil a foothold. Thank you for all You are doing in my life.

In Jesus' Name, ————————————

Amen

Serving

At this time you should be attending and connecting with a local church. Your relationship and dependency upon Jesus should be growing in trust and love. You should also be experiencing breakthroughs, moving you into the arena of victory. God is doing a great work in you and He is not finished yet! It is time to start shining. One of the greatest boosts for a person's self-image can be to start serving and making a difference in other people's lives. Serving also takes the focus off of your problem while serving. God created you to glorify His name!

Mark 10:44-45 "(44) And whosoever of you will be the chiefest, shall be servant of all. (45) For even the Son of man came not to be ministered unto, but to minister, and to give his life a ransom for many."

1 Peter 4:10 As every man hath received the gift, even so minister the same one to another, as good stewards of the manifold grace of God.

Read 1 Corinthians Chapter 12.

It is time that you serve others and realize life is not just about you. Life is about caring for others as Christ has cared for you. God has placed many people in your life to bring you where you are. God says that now that you have received blessings, it is time to serve. God does not give restoration, healing, transformation and truth so that you can just keep it for yourself. God reveals and graciously gives this blessing so that you can gladly give it away to others. When you surrendered to Jesus, God gave you a supernatural gift that you can utilize to serve with passion and joy.

1) Read 1 Corinthians 12 again, and as you read, list the gifts stated.

2) How and why is it important for all the gifts to work together?

3) 1 Corinthians uses the body to explain the gifts. In your own words, how do the gifts work as a body for the kingdom of God?

You are a part of this body of believers that makes up the church. The body moves together, and the church uses all the gifts together. One is not more important than the others—all the gifts must be working together. You have a gift, and it is time to explore and find your supernatural gift and join the body in its work.

➤ LIFE CHANGER #11

1) Find a spiritual gift assessment to study, complete, and discover your special gifts.

2) Connect with a person in leadership at your church to begin exploring where you can start serving to use your gifts.

3) Choose a ministry you are passionate about and start serving for the glory of God!

Prayer

Lord, I want to serve You. Show me who I am and how You have designed me. Open my eyes to Your leading. Open my heart to understand the gifts that you have given me. I am a child of the King and my heart's desire is to glorify Your name by leading others into the freedom and truth of Jesus Christ. Thank You for gifting me so miraculously.

In Jesus' Name, _____

Amen

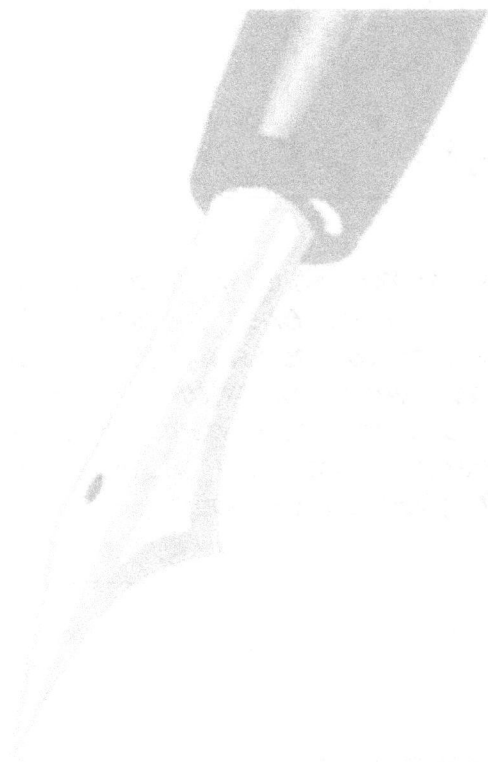

Tell Your Story

I am praying that at this time God's Holy Spirit has healed, moved, and released you from the darkness of defeat into the light of victory. It has been a long journey of looking deep inside your heart and exchanging the death of lies for the truth of freedom. YOU HAVE A STORY TO TELL! Your story is God's testimony of His grace, power, and glory! Without God you would have never been able to have the freedom that you have now. Others need this same hope and freedom. Others need to hear that they are not alone in their battles with defeat.

A testimony is evidence that a witness bears and testifies of its existence. Testimonies in the name of Christ are evidence that Jesus is alive and active in our world. You are giving your testimony as a witness that God is all-powerful and He is the one who gave you hope, perseverance, strength, and power to claim victory. In giving your story, share where you began, how God changed you each step of the way, and where you are today. You are now called to share your story to set other captives free—you hold the key!

1 Peter 3:15 "But sanctify the Lord God in your hearts: and be ready always to give an answer to every man that asketh you a reason of the hope that is in you with meekness and fear"

Psalms 119:27 "Make me to understand the way of thy precepts: so shall I talk of thy wondrous works."

1 Corinthians 1:6 "Even as the testimony of Christ was confirmed in you"

Your testimony is hope to those who have no hope. Your story, your struggle—these same issues are waging war against someone else. Others need to hear that they are not alone, but that someone understands the struggle. They need to hear that you battled the same war and prevailed. You can relate to their pain, hurt, and the chains that are keeping them shackled.

If one did not experience a certain life situation, one cannot fully comprehend it. For example, if I did not lose a parent, I could have sympathy for one who did; but, I could not fully understand the emotions and healing process involved. If I have lost a parent, I can understand the emptiness, the loss, and the pain. I can then relate and understand fully when someone loses a parent. It is the same with your story: it can encourage another that you understand, you fought, and with the power of the Holy Spirit, they can also have victory! You are now a life saver to the one who is dying.

It is time to tell your story!

➢ LIFE CHANGER #12

1) Write your testimony, making it no longer than four minutes long. Remember to share where you were, how Jesus gave you strength and victory, and where you are today.

2) Practice reading your testimony so that you know it seamlessly.

3) Share your testimony with others who may need to hear it.

➢ LIFE CHANGER: UPDATE

Second Half of the Journey

At this point, you should have completed the following life changes:

1) Forgive yourself: Confess your sins and apologize to those you have offended.

2) Forgive others: Ask God to start healing your heart to forgive, write a letter releasing the person who wronged you, and release the wrong they have done by forgiving them. Continue to pray for that person or persons, and ask God to bless them.

3) Deal with your anger: Write what ignites your anger, how you respond to it, how negative responses affect your life, and how you could respond positively. Pray over your anger and begin to release positive responses when your anger ignites.

4) Serve others: Take a spiritual gift assessment, connect with leadership to explore areas to serve, and begin serving with a joyful heart.

5) Tell your story: write and share your testimony.

Conclusion

You have now completed the Life Change process! These life changes may take reviewing, and you may have to repeat some of the life changers. Life change can happen quickly, or it may take months. The key to success is not how quickly the transformation occurs. Success is found simply in the fact that transformation is occurring. The severity of the battle you are fighting will dictate if transformation is obtained quickly or at a slower pace.

Another factor that influences how quickly victory is obtained is as I stated at the beginning of the book: This is not a curriculum, nor is it to be used as such. This is not a quick fix-it or a how-to book. This coaching book was designed to move you into a dynamic relationship, fully depending on the power of the Holy Spirit and God's written Word. Doing the life change exercises without seeking the transforming power and relationship of Jesus Christ will not produce change. Freedom comes only by the truth and power of the living God.

As long as you breathe, the enemy will try to drag you back into the prison of defeat. Feel free to reflect back to this life-changing book to point you in the right direction: straight into the arms of Jesus. Cling to God and the devil must flee. Run from the devil and embrace God, and you will live life in victory! You choose life or death, blessing or curses; circumstances and people do not! Seek first the kingdom of God and love God with all your heart, soul, and mind. Remember to obey Him—Jesus is the way, the truth and the life—please choose life!

Prayer

Lord, please cover me with Your grace and Your mercy. This road of life is not always easy; in fact, it is sometimes very hard. Please teach me to lean on You during the tough times, and continue to support me along the way. I need Your power to fight the spiritual battle that rages on and causes turmoil in my life. I need to forgive, release defeat, and choose to walk in Your way. Help me to take what I've learned and use it to change someone else's life the way You are still changing mine. I thank You so much for Your great love.

In Jesus' Name,   _____

Amen

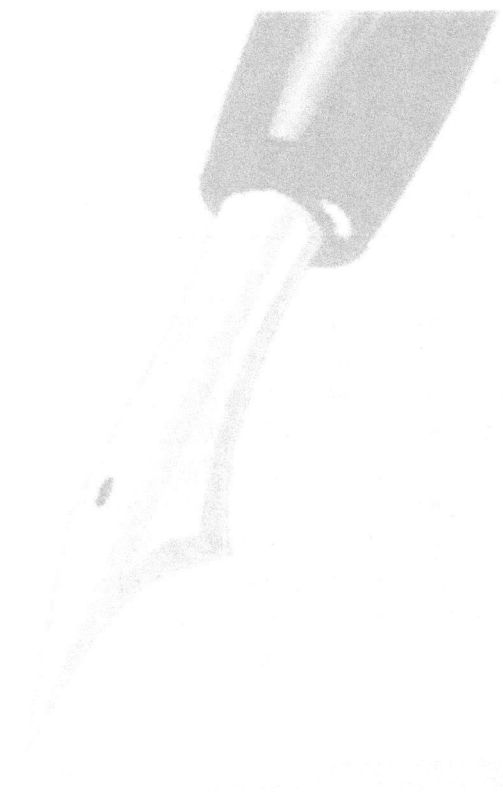

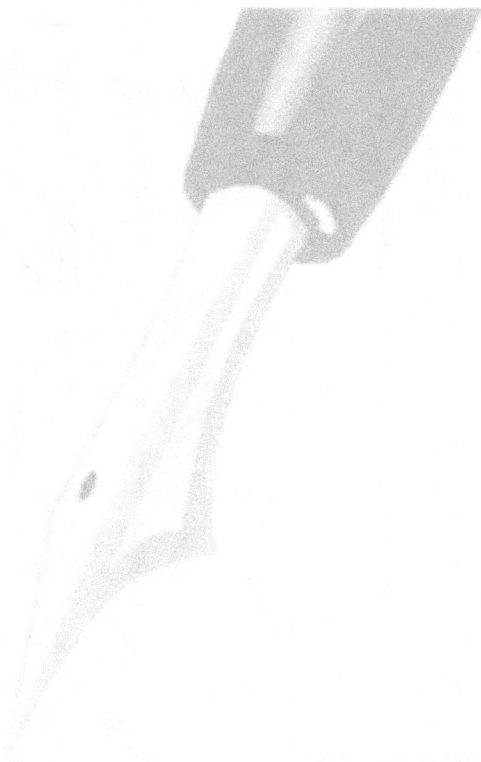